Communications In Nature

Carsten R. Jorgensen

Written and published in Canada.

ISBN-13: 978-0-9949338-8-1

DEDICATION

This book is dedicated to all the animals I have known.

CONTENTS

ACKNOWLEDGMENTS

I am very grateful to my daughter Dana Woodard for editing and for her helpful suggestions.

All images in this book are known or thought to be public domain.

Cover Design by Dana Woodard with special thanks to
Petra (Pezibear)
from pixabay.com for providing the images used to make the cover.

1. INTRODUCTION

All living things communicate. Some communications go unnoticed by humans. However, some communications are found to be astonishing when they are noticed. Humans who have pets know that their pets communicate. Cats purr, dogs wag their tails. These animals also use other means of communicating.

Some humans talk to their plants. They claim that these plants react to their conversations.

Humans are very good at communicating. One reason for this is that we have vocal cords which is lacking in other mammals. We also use body language and signs. We developed reading and writing. Later came radio and television. Sound recordings and pictures were also developed. Now we use computers, cell phones and moving pictures (movies, YouTube, etc.)

Nature also has an extensive range of ways to communicate; many of which we are only just beginning to discover. As we continue to learn more about how things communicate, we may be able to better understand the world around us and what parts we play in nature's grand social network.

2. DNA

Internal communications are constantly taking place in all living things. This is done by the DNA (deoxyribonucleic acid). This is the hereditary material in every cell of the organism. The DNA is a code made up of four chemical bases: Adenine (A), Guanine (G), Cytosine (C), and Thymine (T). Human DNA consists of about 3 billion bases and more than 99% are the same in all people.

The order and sequences of the DNA bases communicates with the organism on how to build and maintain its body. This includes cells, hormones, physical characteristics, enzymes, and anti bodies.

Dogs and humans share 84% of their genes and about 98% of our genes are the same as chimpanzees. Our DNA is more than 60% identical with chickens, 60 % identical with bananas, and 60% identical with fruit flies.

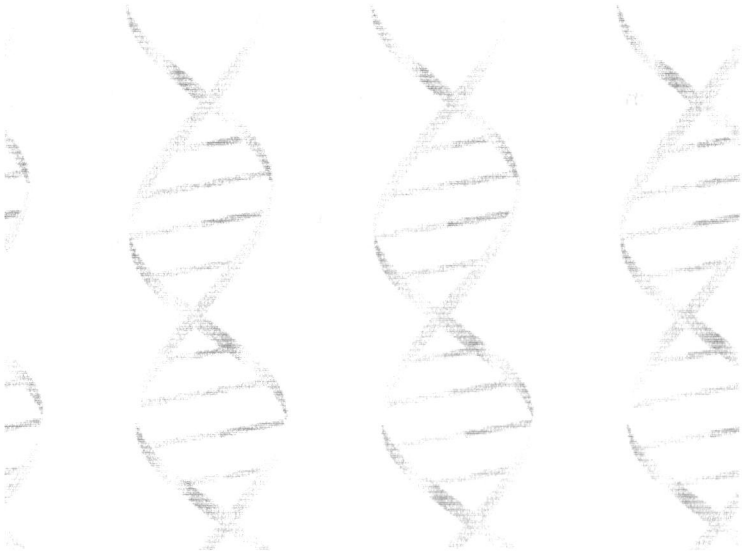

A strand of DNA

3. BACTERIA

Many people in our society have a paranoia about bacteria. They view bacteria as the enemy and that it must be destroyed. However, bacteria helps humans. There are bacteria living in our mouth, nose, throat, and intestines. Although they have no sense organs, they can detect chemicals and also have the sense of touch. Thus, they communicate.

Humans can not digest all the food we eat. Bacteria eat the indigestible carbohydrates and digest it for us. We would be unable to survive without our bacteria because we would be unable to digest the indigestible carbohydrates. Our relationship with our bacteria is called a symbiotic relationship.

Our bacteria also attacks harmful microbes and keeps them from taking up space. Our intestinal bacteria have a strong effect in enhancing our immune system. Our immune systems are needed to avoid inflammatory responses to antigens and to avoid hostile bacteria while defending the body. Enzymes, which we need for digestion, are produced by our bacteria. Our bacteria also manufacture vitamin K.

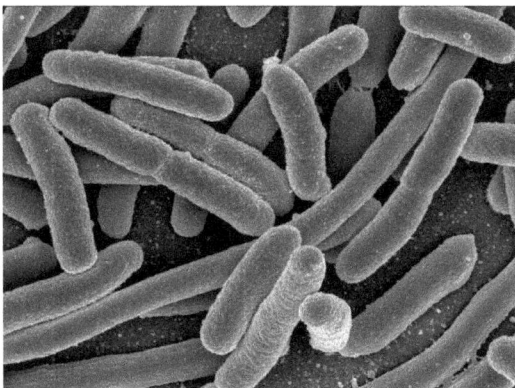

A group of bacteria

Sometimes a human has too few symbiotic bacteria. This is usually caused by taking antibiotics. The situation is usually corrected by ingesting these symbiotic bacteria. These bacteria are sold in some health stores where they are called probiotics. The probiotics are sold in capsules so that the bacteria are not destroyed in the mouth and esophagus on their way to the digestive system. Another way to regain the necessary bacteria is to eat organic yogurt.

It has been determined that 90% of bacteria are not harmful. These 90% are, in fact, beneficial.

Beneficial bacteria in our world carry out many tasks. Nitrogen makes up part of the protein molecules. Nitrogen is essential for all life. The plants known as legumes have nodules on their roots which fixate nitrogen from the air and makes it available for the plant to absorb into its system. These nodules are colonies of bacteria which are able to absorb the nitrogen for the plant. Nitrogen fixing bacteria, which enable a tree to use nitrogen, are found on the branches of the tree.

At the University of Wisconsin Health Sciences scientists are studying how bacteria perceive and respond to changes in their environment.

Bacteria respond to their environment by talking to each other using a form of chemical communication called quorum sensing. As more and more bacteria secrete the signal molecule, it can result in activating specific genetic pathways resulting in such actions as, for example, secreting toxins or forming a protective biofilm.

Scientists from the University of Groningen, in the Netherlands, have succeeded in incorporating a light-controlled switch into a molecule used by bacteria for quorum sensing. This is a process by which bacteria communicate and subsequently control different cellular processes. Cells are constantly in communication with each other. They do this by secreting proteins. When those proteins reach other cells, it changes the cells' behavior. With the molecule described, it is possible to either inhibit or stimulate communication.

The scientists were able to find a compound which strongly inhibited the quorum sensing after irradiating it with light. They also found that they could strongly stimulate it to increase the quorum sensing sometimes to as much as 700 times the normal rate.

4. VIRUSES

In 1892, Dmitri Ivanovsky described a small infectious non-bacterial agent infecting the tobacco plant. This small agent was a virus. There are millions of types of viruses found in every ecosystem. They infect all types of organisms from animals to plants to microorganisms.

While not inside a cell or attempting to break into a cell each virus exists as a small independent thing. Each virus consists of a strand of RNA (ribonucleic acid) or DNA (deoxyribonucleic acid) The RNA or DNA is encased in a protein molecule. Biologists are still debating about whether a virus is alive or not.

Does a virus communicate? Well, doctors call them communicable diseases. There is no evidence that viruses communicate. When it has entered a living cell, the virus uses material from the cell's own plasma to reproduce itself. After many reproductions, the viruses break out of the cell much to the discomfort of the host. In humans, viruses have caused smallpox, the common cold, all types of flu, measles, mumps, rubella, chicken pox, shingles, hepatitis, herpes, cold sores, polio, rabies, Ebola, and Hantu fever.

It has now been proposed that viruses eavesdrop on their host cells in order to determine when is the best time to make its attack on surrounding bacterial cells. Entering other cells is the only way they can survive.

The bacterial cells communicate, using quorum sensing, to figure out how many other bacteria are in the vicinity, allowing them to act as a group and increase the power of disease-causing bacteria to do damage. The virus listens and when it hears that there is a large enough quantity of bacteria in the vicinity, it knows that it is time to strike.

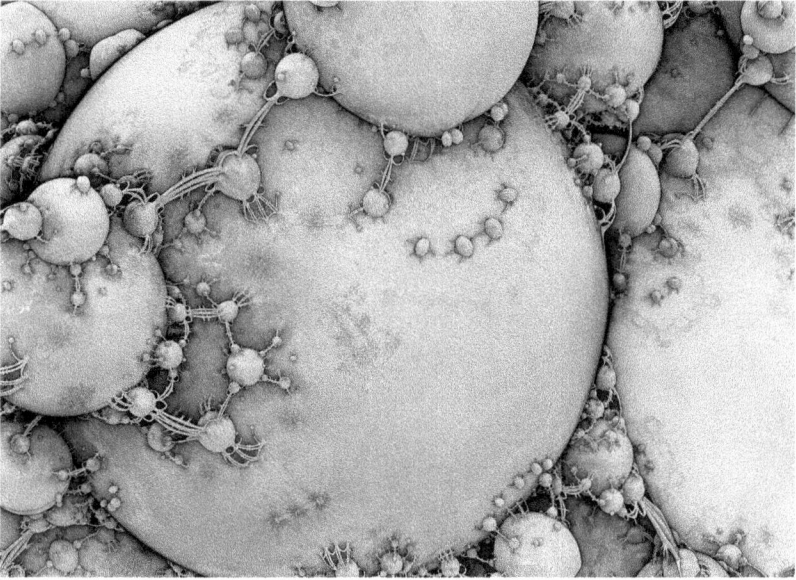

When there are enough bacteria the virus will strike

There are no vaccinations for bacteria, but scientists have developed vaccinations for viruses. For a whole population to have protection from a disease at least 80% must be vaccinated. The 20% not vaccinated are protected by what is known as herd protection. These individuals are still at risk but the chances of them becoming infected is greatly reduced because most of the individuals they meet are immune due to being vaccinated.

5. WATER

How does water detect its environment and the living beings in it? Is water capable of detecting what is around it? Does it have emotions?

Dr. Masaru Emoto, a Japanese scientist studied how the molecular structure in water transforms when it is subjected to human words, sounds, and intentions. Working with water in glass jars, he demonstrated how water exposed to loving, pleasant, benevolent, and compassionate sounds resulted in pleasing and beautiful molecular formations while water subjected to fearful and discordant sounds resulted in ugly, disconnected, fractured molecular formations.

Dr. Emoto was heavily criticized by other scientists. They found that he did not have any controls which is required in the scientific method. Controls are always needed to ensure that the observed effects are not caused by something else. Some of Dr. Emoto's tests involved jars of water which also contained rice. It would seem that he was not using distilled water. I suspect that his results were due to microorganisms in the water he used.

6. PLANTS

Jack C. Schultz has stated that "plants are just very slow animals."

He has also stated that "if you make a very fast movie of a growing plant you will see an animal".

Plants perceive the world without eyes, ears or brains. Plants fight for territory, evade predators, and trap prey, and like animals, they exhibit behaviour. The woodland sequence from David Attenborough's Life series has shown this.

These plants are moving with a purpose which means they must be aware of what is going on around them. Appel and Crocroft found that the sound of a munching caterpillar caused plants to flood their leaves with chemical defenses to ward off attackers.

A munching caterpillar

Plants hear, see, smell and detect what is around them. They move (extremely slowly). They act just like animals. Consuelo

De Moraes of the Swiss Federal Institute of Technology in Zurich has shown that the parasitic plant known as the dodder vine sniffs out a potential host. The dodder plant then wriggles through the air. When it reaches its host, it coils itself around it to extract its nutrients.

A dodder plant surrounding a host

Not only are plants aware of their surroundings they also have feelings. Plants that hear their humans talking to them thrive better. They also perk up when hearing classical music such as Mozart. If they hear music from rock bands, they become depressed and do poorly. Plants like to be loved.

Plants communicate to other life forms. Their reproductive parts become flowers which look beautiful and have a sweet scent. These flowers attract insects which go from flower to flower to eat or collect nectar. The nectar is the plants reward to the insect for helping them out. The insect also picks up pollen which, when distributed to other flowers, cause these plants to reproduce.

After the flowering stage is over, the flower turns into a fruiting body, often a berry (strawberries, blueberries, etc.). The berries take on a brilliant colour; most often red. This is the plant communicating to birds, chipmunks, squirrels, rodents and other animals. The plant wants the other life forms to eat its berries.

Raspberry, strawberry, and cherry

Thus, the seeds of these plants wind up in the digestive systems of these living beings.

Blueberries and raspberries

The seeds pass out of the bodies in the excrement. The seeds are thus naturally fertilized and are able to start life in a new location. Humans have played a scam on these plants by using septic systems.

7. TREES

Trees, like all plants, perceive the world without eyes, ears or brains. They fight for territory, evade predators, and, like animals, they exhibit behaviour.

Trees are loving beings. When my wife and I go into a forest we have a loving peaceful feeling which is provided by the trees. Many other people have experienced these feelings while canoeing, camping, and walking forest trails. Some of these people have formed environmental groups dedicated to protecting trees. Other people call these tree loving people "Tree Huggers".

Trees are loving beings

Trees reach out to us in many ways. They invite us to tune in to their stillness; to listen more carefully.

History is rich in stories of people conversing with trees.

The rustling of the leaves on an oak tree was regarded as the voice of Zeus. In the book Shahnameh by Firdawsi, Alexander the Great visited a talking tree. Druids were said to be able to consult oak trees for divinatory purposes, as were the Streghe with Rowan trees. Many don't take stories like these seriously. Thomas Berry, an ecotheologian, notes that "We experience the world as a collection of objects, no longer as a communion of subjects".

Even if we don't communicate with trees, the trees communicate with each other. When a tree is cut down, the nearby trees are in mortal fear for their lives. Science suggests trees are intrinsically social beings.

VIB researchers at Ghent University in Belgium are studying Trees and their symbiotic relationships with mycorrhizal fungi; thin filaments that connect an estimated 90% of land plants. Trees grow better with certain symbiotic fungi occurring in their root systems. The fungus facilitates the uptake of scarce nutrients such as phosphates and nitrogen. They also protect the trees from parasites found in the soil.

Some fungi associated with tree roots connect one tree root to other tree roots with their tendrils. These are used by the trees to subtly converse with one another underground, just like people use telephone land lines. Researchers consider this to be the "Wood Wide Web".

These kinds of connections might be more typical among trees than once suspected. While trees may seem like solitary individuals above ground, they are very much connected underground.

Adult trees can share nutrients, carbon, and sugars to more youthful trees. Sick trees can send their remaining nutrients back into the system for other trees to use. And they can speak with one another about dangers such as insect infestations. A plant under attack from aphids can indicate to a nearby plant that it should raise its defensive response before the aphids reach it.

It has been known for some time that plants communicate above ground in comparable ways, by means of airborne hormones. But such warnings are more precise in terms of source and recipient when sent by means of the Wood Wide Web.

The discovery of the Wood Wide Web's presence, and our expanding understanding of how it works and it's functions, brings up more questions. Is a woodland better envisioned as one large super organism instead of a group of individualistic ones? Where does a species start and end? Do trees have friendships and do they have a social life?

There are debates over the Wood Wide Web which suggest that there is two competing visions of the network: the socialist forest, in which trees act as caregivers to one another, with the well-off supporting the needy, and the capitalist forest, in which all entities are acting out of self-interest within a competitive system.

Two ecologists hiking in a rain forest near Auckland, New Zealand, came across a tree stump that was still alive. It was a leafless kauri tree stump rising a few feet off the ground.
(The biggest kauri tree is known as the Tane Mahuta or the Lord of the Forest. It is 168 feet high with a 115 foot canopy).
The ecologists looked closely at the tree stump and could see living tissue. It was clearly not dead.

They found that the kauri stump lives due to the neighbouring trees imparting water to it. The trees have an underground root connection that may have formed long before the tree had ever became a stump. Why would a tree support a stump that can't reproduce or make its own food? And for the stump, why bother to continue to interact with the living trees around it? Are these social aspects? Or are they competitive aspects?

This kauri tree stump is not an isolated incident. Naturalists have observed living tree stumps in New Jersey, Sierra Nevada, British Columbia and other places.

Like all other plants, trees also move. They do not move as fast as Treebeard and his friends in the story of "The Lord of The Rings". Like other plants, trees move with a purpose. A tree has been recorded close to a fence with one branch resting on the fence. Over a long time (days) the tree lifted the branch so that it was not resting on the fence. Thus, the branch was not being rubbed by the fence during high winds.

8. INSECTS

Insects have compound eyes but they see only one view. Their brain compensates and one picture is formed for them. However, their field of vision is much greater than that of mammals and birds. The insect's brain works so fast that it perceives motion as slow motion. Their vision is good at detecting movement. It has been found that insects see colour but not as well as humans.

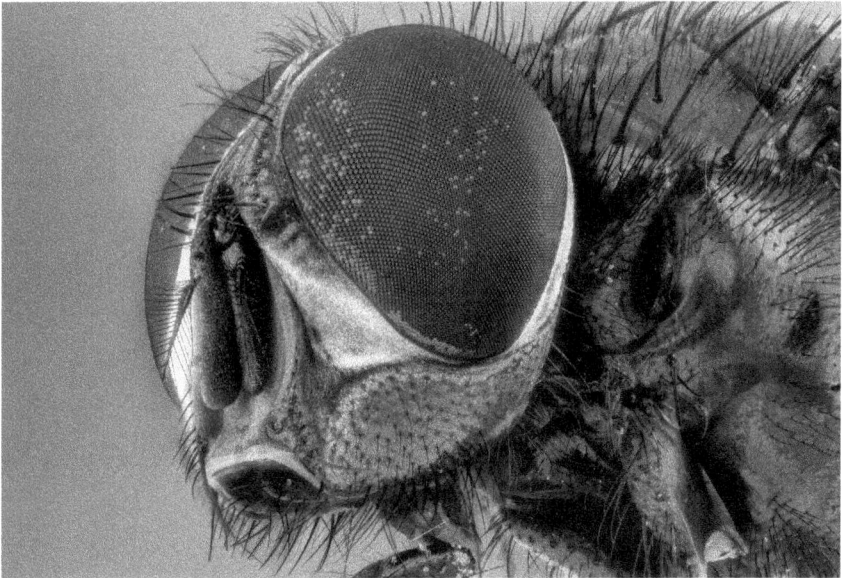

Insects have compound eyes

Most people think of insects as little automatons acting on instinct But researchers of the National Academy of Science have discovered that insects have the capacity for the most basic aspect of consciousness; subjective experience. Andrew Barron of Australia's Macquarie University suggests that invertebrates could be motivated by subjective experience, which is the very beginning of consciousness. An insect does not act on all its sensory cues. Instead, it selects what is most relevant to it at the time and acts on that.

Klein and Barron state that in vertebrates, the mid-brain is responsible for the basic capacity for subjective experience. The cortex forms much of what we are aware of, but the mid-brain is what makes us capable of being aware. Mapping of insect brains have shown that their central nervous system performs the same function as the mid brain in larger animals. Thus, insects are conscious. They are aware of many things but not all things.

Insects communicate by sight, touch, sounds, and scent. Insects can even detect stimuli that are outside of our sensory scope. For example, butterflies can see ultraviolet wavelengths and bees can detect the plane of polarization of light. Cockroaches can see the radiation from radioactive isotopes.

Experiments with thrips show that they can detect solar UVB radiation. The thrips not only preferred leaves from plants that were not exposed to solar UVB over leaves from UVB-exposed plants in laboratory and field choice experiments, but they also appeared to directly sense and avoid exposure to solar UVB.

An example of scent communication is the luna moth. When ready to breed, the luna female flies into the air and emits a scent. The males can detect the female's scent from over two miles away.

Luna Moth

Bees fly out and search for the closest flowers from which to gather nectar. When such a scout bee has found suitable flowers it flies back to the hive. There, the bee performs a dance while other bees watch. The dance tells the other bees how far it is to the flowers and the shortest direction to get there. The scout also gives the other bees a taste of the nectar which it has collected from the flowers.

Australian scientists have announced that bees can learn how to add and subtract. Dr. Adrian Dyer, co-author of the research, stated that not every bee could do this automatically but, they were able to teach them how to do it. The bees were found to be better with numbers than many human children.

Honey bees were found to have a notion of the concept of the number zero which is a notion many human children find very difficult to learn. Researchers from RMIT at the University of Melbourne have demonstrated that bees consider zero a number. The researchers were unclear as to why bees would do that.

Ants belong to the same Order called Hymenoptera. It is estimated that there are 22,000 species of ants. They live in colonies. Some live in small colonies of about a dozen to 20 members while others live in a vast territory with millions of members.

Black Ant

When I was a school boy, in grade 7, I noticed that the grass covered school yard contained black ants. The whole school yard had numerous tiny mounds from which ants came and went.

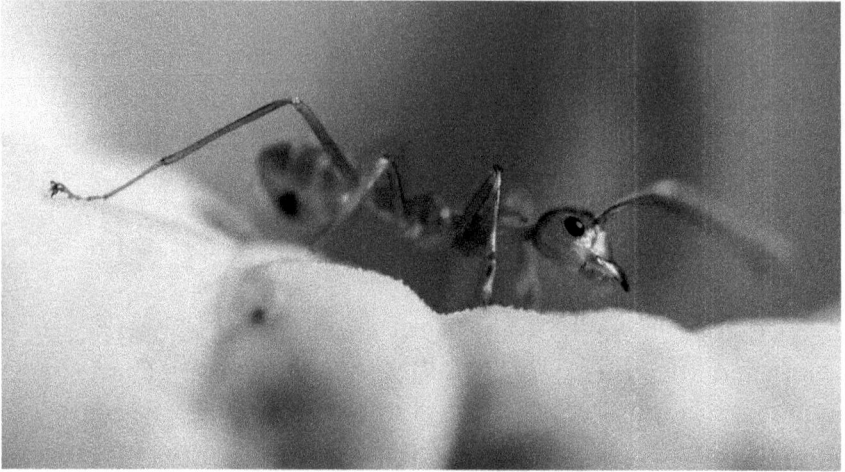

Red Ant

One day red ants appeared. There were so many that the whole school yard was now covered with both red and black ants. Before I left to go home I took a close look at all those ants. The red ants were fighting the black ants. It was like a great war.

When I arrived at school the next morning, the school yard was covered with dead ants all lying close together. The red ants and the black ants had killed each other. The number of ant bodies in such a large field was amazing.

The different species of ants make a living in different ways. Some ants hunt insects which they kill and carry home to their nests. There is a species of ants that uses other ants as slaves. They raid the nests of other ant species and take the eggs which they carry home to their nests. The hatching ants become their slaves and have to do all the work. When these ants kill insects the slaves have to carry the prey back to the nest.

There are ants that keep aphids (plant lice) and get their food by milking the aphids just like humans milk cows and goats. The aphids are carried out in the morning and placed on the leaves of plants. In the evening the ants go out and pick up their aphids and carry them back to the nest.

Ants tending their aphids

In South and Central America, Mexico, and southern United States, there live leaf cutter ants. There are 47 species of leaf cutter ants. These ants are farmers. They go out and cut leaves which they carry home to their nest. There, they further treat the leaves to make them into a mulch on which they grow a fungus. This fungus is their food.

There have been some very large ant colonies. On the northernmost of the main islands of Japan, the island Hokkaido, was found an ant colony covering 670 acres. It had one million queens and 325 million worker ants; about the same as the population of humans in the U.S.A. The very largest ant colony ever found was in southern Europe. It covered 3,700 miles of coast and contained uncounted billions of ants. Jeffrey Kluger has pointed out that technically these are not single colonies but a series of them that have overlapped.

Each species of insect has its own means of communicating. From the lights of fire flies to the chirping of crickets, the communication abilities of insects are amazing.

A Wasp

It has been thought that the use of logic was confined to animals with complex nervous systems. But a group of scientists have found that wasps can use a kind of logical deduction. This was reported by Chelsea Whyte.

The logic used by wasps is called transitive inference. This was the first use of logic discovered in invertebrates. Tibbet in the Journal of the Royal Society of Biological Letters has hypothesized that wasps have evolved this ability because they spend a great deal of time fighting over dominance. Transitive inference is really important in figuring out dominance.

A Hornet

An investigation of honey bees showed that these insects did not possess transitive inference.

9. DOMESTICATED INSECTS

In antiquity, the Chinese kept insects as pets. Examples include cicadas and grasshoppers. The favourite pet insect was the cricket. They were initially kept because of their songs. The people loved the sounds of the crickets. They were kept in gourds which enhanced the volume of the cricket songs. There are Chinese houses which house so many crickets in gourds that humans can not stand to be in the house because of the tremendous racket of the crickets.

In some places in China, people enjoy watching crickets fight. Cricket fights are staged as public entertainment and there is heavy betting on the outcome of a match. Development of an embryo to adult cricket takes from one to two months. Then, the adult lives for about one month. Therefore, cricket owners must often seek new crickets as fighters and breeders.

Cricket fighting tournaments started in the 19th century. In Shanghai, the fighters are sorted into 9 weight classes, from 0.51 to 0.74 grams.

A cricket fight usually ended in the death of the loser. The winner would bite off the loser's head. In the twentieth century, this changed and the loser would be allowed to retreat.

The highest price for a single cricket champion fighter has been recorded as $12,000.00 in 1999. The people of Whampoa buried their dead fighting champions in tiny silver coffins.

A Cricket

Another insect domesticated by the Chinese are the praying mantis (or preying mantis).

The praying mantis is well known as an eater of grasshoppers. It will catch a grasshopper in its two front legs and chew on it like we chew on a cob of corn. It will also eat any other insect it comes across. It is not particular about what it eats. After breeding, the female often eats the smaller male. The mantis is a large insect. Some people have observed them eating small animals like mice and moles. There is even a record of a humming bird being eaten by a praying mantis.

A praying mantis

The Chinese sometimes take their praying mantis pet on a walk with a string acting as a leash. At this time, people in North America are now keeping praying mantises as pets.

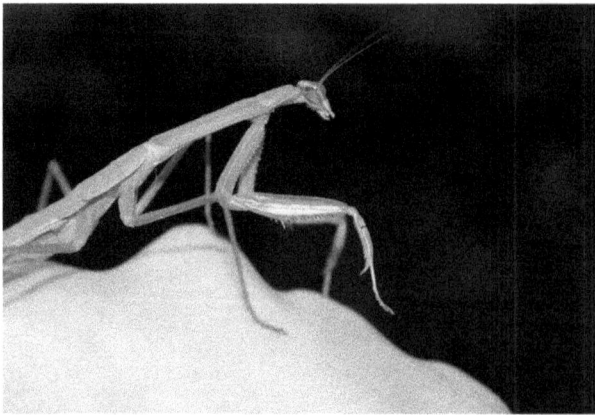

Praying mantis on a human fist

Some people keep beetles and others keep ants. The ants are usually kept in a glass cage, called a formicarium where people can see the ants running through the corridors of their nest.

A formicarium inside an aquarium

The Chinese are famous for silk. They domesticated the silk moth.

A silk moth

The silk moth larvae spins a cocoon. The thread used to make the cocoon is made of a protein structure. This protein is silk. The silk cocoon is harvested. The heat and water used to harvest the silk kills the larvae and it is usually eaten.

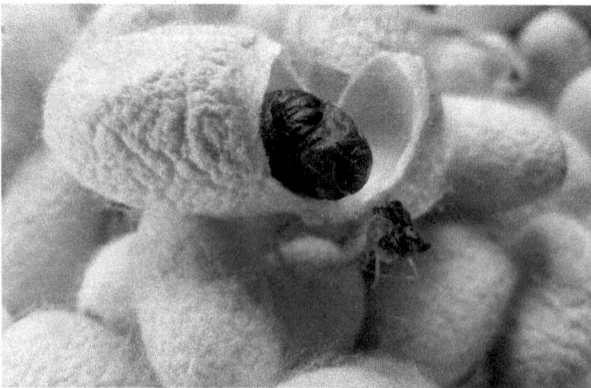

Silkworm cocoons

Honey bees were domesticated in ancient Greece and in ancient Egypt. Today bees are kept not only for their honey but also as pollinators for domestic plants including vineyards, orchards and other agricultural plants. In Toronto, Ontario, there are countless bee hives kept on roof tops of high rise apartment buildings. On these same roof tops people grow agricultural plants. However, in other places such as North Bay, Ontario, domestic bees are not allowed. North Bay has a statute classifying domestic bees as farm animals.

A bee hive in an aviary

10. MY ENCOUNTERS WITH BUMBLE BEES

As a 13-year-old boy living on my parents' farm I had a few incidents of bumble bees communicating with me. The first time I was in a field by myself. I saw a wild flower near the fence. I went over to look at the flower. It was beautiful. I squatted for a closer look. A bumble bee arrived and entered the flower. I moved a bit closer to observe what the bumble bee was doing. Bumble bees normally ignore humans.

Bumble bee in a flower

The bumble bee seemed aware of what I was doing. It left the flower and hovered slightly above the flower and seemed to be watching me. Its humming changed to a slightly lower pitch. I suddenly had the impression that this bee was giving me a warning. Then, the bumble bee surprised me by flying into my face and stinging me.

On the farm we used to take in hay and straw by loading it by pitch fork onto a horse drawn wagon. Later our neighbour,

George Jones bought an International harvester. This harvester was used in the fields to harvest grain. The grain was deposited into burlap bags. Then, the harvester was driven to the barn where the straw was blown into the barn.

A harvester in a grain field

One day, I was helping my father and George Jones with the harvesting. When we got to the barn, George set the harvester to blow the straw into the barn. A huge amount of straw hit a bumblebee nest. A swarm of angry bumblebees came roaring out of the barn and attacked me. They went for my face and stung me many times. I ran into the house where my mother killed a few of the bees who had accompanied me. Female bumble bees are able to sting repeatedly.

To this day I still wonder why I was the one attacked. They left George and my dad alone. It has occurred to me that maybe the bumblebee from the flower was one of them. Maybe, they picked on me because that one remembered me from the flower incident and told the others about me.

11. FISH

Like all animals, fish need to know what is going on around them. They have the five senses that people have: hearing, sight, touch, smell, and taste. They also have a sixth sense. This is the lateral line which runs along each side of the fish. It enables them to detect vibrations in the water.

Some fish also have a seventh sense. These fish are able to detect electric currents. Water dissolves electrolytes, therefore, there are always electric currents in the water where fish live. They live in an electrolyte solution.

Fish communicate with one another. They "talk" by vibrating their swim bladder, thus making a sound. Most fish make sounds too low for the human ear to hear. Their talk includes grunts, chirps, and pops. However, some fish, like the Grunt and the Drum, are able to make sounds that humans can hear. In fact, this is how the Grunt and the Drum got their names.

Fish communicate with each other for different reasons. These include attracting a mate, scaring off predators, and orienting themselves.

The gunnard species have a wide variety of vocal sounds, and they keep up a constant chatter. Cod are usually silent except when they are spawning. Some damselfish make threatening sounds to try to scare off predators. The damselfish also make these sounds at divers in an attempt to scare them off.

Goldfish have excellent hearing but you can not have a conversation with them. They cannot make any noise.

Fish with electrical organs communicate with electrical impulses for social reasons. These electrical organs are also used to warn off trespassers.

Many deep sea fish are able to chemically produce bioluminescence which they use to communicate certain information such as species recognition, courtship, attack warning, and submission.

12. REPTILES

Dr. Sharman Hoppes, clinical assistant professor of the Texas A&M College of Veterinary Medicine and Biomedical Science, claims that reptiles demonstrate basic emotions. The two main ones are fear and aggression. They also exhibit pleasure when fed by their owners.

Lizards and tortoises appear to like some people more than others. When being petted, a tortoise will stick its neck out and close its eyes thus appearing to enjoy the encounter. This is also the case with lizards.

Many people are uncomfortable around reptiles, specially snakes. During my last year in public school, I was selected to give a five-minute speech in a competition. I elected to talk about snakes. I spent hours writing my speech. When I presented it at home, my mother did not like it. Instead, she helped me to write a speech about dogs (much more appreciated by people).

The speech competition involved many rural schools. I placed second. The winner was a girl from my class and also from my school. She spoke about the cow. The speech began "They strolled down the lane together. The sky, it was sprinkled with stars. They reached the old gate in silence, and he lifted for her the bars. But she never smiled nor thanked him. For she knew not how. He was just the farmer's son, and she was their faithful cow."

The speech went on to describe what would happen if the cow was removed from the globe (our planet).

Grass Snake

Snakes are solitary creatures. They cannot hear air borne sound. They do not have much intraspecific communication. But they do have some communication which they use to find and defend breeding partners.

Snakes have the sense of smell. They do this with their tongue. A snake will stick out its tongue and draw it back inside its mouth. This is how they smell. This is used to locate their prey.

Emerald Lizard

Lizards communicate with each other. Their modes of communication include visual, chemical, tactile and vocal. Some lizards use only one mode while the other species use two or more.

13. MAMMALS

Many people experience revulsion when confronted with spiders and insects. Humans are more comfortable with birds and mammals.

Mammals communicate using sound, scent, and sight. Sound vocalizes communications. The scent of scat marks a territory. Sight is used to detect body language.

People who own animals, talk to them on occasion. When we ramble on in a sentence after sentence, our pet has no comprehension of what we are talking about. Therefore, the conversation is usually one way – us to them.

Humans are just as confused about animals talking. We hear barks, yelps, squeaks, and chirps. But usually humans have no idea what these animals are talking about in their carefully organized and grammatically correct sentences.

There is however, some amount of understanding. Dogs can learn to understand the words: sit, stay, come, bad, fetch, go, no. When they understand those, then "That is a good puppy!"

Fetch

Mammals communicate complicated things without saying a word. They use body language. Dogs communicate with each other using body language, some of which takes less than a second. Patricia McConnell, an animal behaviorist and adjunct professor of zoology at the University of Wisconsin-Madison, found that some signals between dogs last only a tenth of a second and involve a change in posture of only a quarter of an inch, and this conveys volumes of information.

Dogs also watch us for our body language. An extremely light lean forward is a warning to stay back. An extremely light lean back is a signal that it is alright to come forward. A few obvious body language signs are actually understood by humans such as the sign that a dog wants to play or that a cat wants food.

I want to play

Most small children are taught that it is impolite to stare. A person on the receiving end of a stare becomes uncomfortable. This is why most people are uncomfortable performing on stage or having to give a public speech. Animals also become uncomfortable when being stared at. When a dog stares at another dog or a cat stares at another cat, it is a challenge. Two things may happen. There is either a violent fight or one backs slowly down. If you stare into the eyes of a parrot, it will bite you.

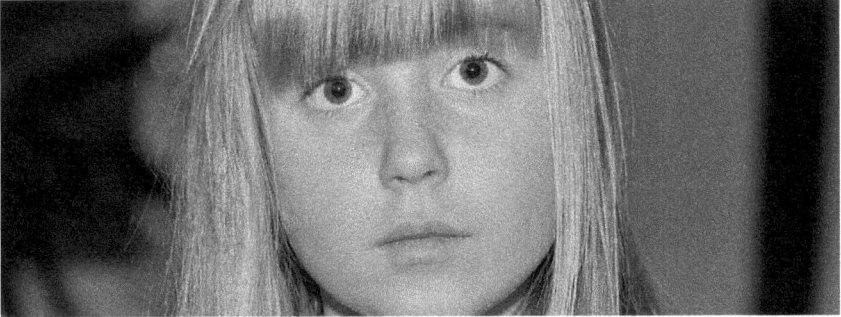

The staring is a mistake often made by people who fear big dogs. The person stares at the big dog. Yes, the dog is now receiving a challenge. The person is already full of adrenaline from fright. He (or she) is in the fight or flight mode. The dog can sense the adrenaline but does not know the mind of the person and, therefore, prepares for the expected action of the human by taking a defensive stance or an offensive stance which further terrifies the human. Yes, it is impolite to stare.

There is a difference when there is a bond between the dog and the human. Then, a stare may have different meanings. It could mean that food is coming. It could mean, "Let's go for a walk." It could mean "Come here and let me pet you."

Wolves hunt in packs. They have been observed hunting deer. Deer are found in their territories called deer yards. These deer do not leave their yard. When chased they stay together for protection. When wolves hunt deer, not all the wolves give chase. Some wolves lie down and rest. Since the deer stay in the deer yard, they eventually run by the same location again. There, the wolves which had been chasing the deer will lie down and rest. The wolves who had been resting get up and continue the chase. This is like a relay race as seen in the Olympics.

Eventually a deer is no longer able to keep up with the herd. This is the one that is attacked and killed. Thus, the weaker and sick deer are culled from the herd. In this way wolves keep deer herds healthy and strong.

A wolf pack

A wolf pack is well-organized because its members communicate a lot with each other.

While we were living at Wasi Lake, in Chisholm Township, Ontario, I was, one day, outside next to the house. I had to pee. I faced away from the house and peed. While I was thus engaged, a very deep growl came from behind me. The growling kept on and also a few snarls. The dog behind me was obviously agitated. I finished, turned around and stared at this dog. It was very big.

The dog kept on growling and baring its teeth. Then, I drew a deep breath and leaning forward. I growled back in a long loud growl. The dog then turned and trotted away up the lane way.

I went into the house and told my wife, Brenda, what had happened. I said that the neighbour's dog had been growling at me. After I described the dog to her, she said, "None of our neighbours have a dog like that. What you saw was a wolf".

What you saw was a wolf.

Another animal that lives and hunts in a pack are the hyena. Most people having watched nature shows on TV and in movies recognize the hyena as a scavenger. They have often shown hyenas lurking at the edge of a lion kill, trying to steal a meal. However, most of the time it is the lions stealing from the hyenas. It is a hyena kill shown on most of these shows which has been stolen by the lions. The hyenas lurking in the background are gathering in an attempt to take back their kill. The hyenas are excellent hunters. The nature shows have lied. It is hard to try to overcome bad gossip.

A spotted hyena

Living in a pack means it is necessary to communicate to your fellow members. Hyenas trying to repel a lion shout out loud whoops to recruit as many members of their clan as they can. As the hyenas get ready for action, they are very nervous. This results in nervous giggles. Humans hear this as laughter. This is where the term laughing hyena came from.

A hyena community is a complex and clever society. It has order, customs, safety, and a sense of community. The society is matrilineal. The very highest ranking male is subordinate to the very lowest ranking female. The males must obey.

Among the females, there is a constant struggle for dominance. The fights are very frequent and very fierce. A group of researchers in Kenya studying a clan observed that just over a few months the dominant female engaged in 117 fights against 19 lower ranked females. They observed 633 fights among all the females.

Another pack hunter is the African wild dog or Cape Hunting Dog. Communication is very important for animals living in packs. In Cape Hunting dog society, the female is the important sex. Puppies eat first, before the adults. As they grow up, it is the young females, not the young males, that leave the pack to start life elsewhere.

Cape Hunting Dog

When we hear animals in nature, we miss a lot of what the animals are saying.

When humans hear a lion roar, we just hear a roar. But, to other lions, there is a lot of information that is vital to the well-being of the pride members in that roar.

Martyn Colbeck, wildlife film maker, has identified 70 distinct vocalizations that elephants make. Everyone knows that elephants make trumpeting sounds. They do this when excited, lost, angry, playful, or surprised. They also make chirps, squeaks, and rumbling sounds. The rumbling sounds are of low frequency and are used to communicate over long distances. Some rumbles are too low to be detected by human ears.

Rumbling conversations

There are other animal communications that we cannot hear. Human range of hearing is 20 to 20,000 Hz. Some animals have sounds above the human range of hearing and some have sounds below human range of hearing. Some elephant rumbles are below the human range of hearing. Bats yell sounds above the human range of hearing.

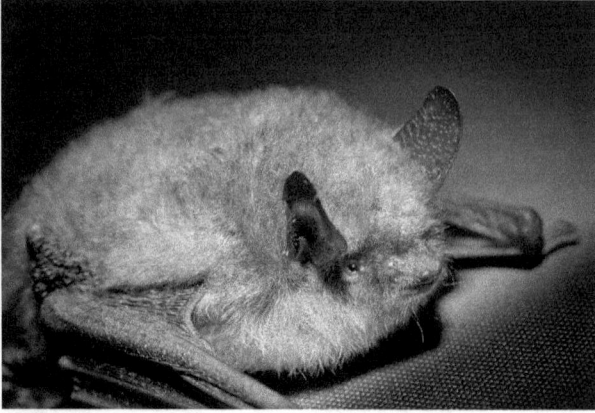

Bats are blind which is remarkable for a flying animal. The bat yells are like radar. The yell bounces off of objects and the bat can hear his location in his environment just like we are visually aware of our location. This technique is called echo location (also called radar). The bats also hunt and catch their prey, mosquitoes and other insects, by using their radar. It is also their means of communicating with each other. Humans can not hear what these creatures are talking about.

Flying bats

Some animals, like whales and dolphins, use echo location to locate food or predators. Their technique is similar to that of the bat. They have an additional advantage over the bat. They can see.

Water is denser than air. Therefore, sound travels much farther in water.

Humpback whale

Bottle nosed dolphins

As well as echo location, these animals also use their sonar to communicate with each other.

14. CATS

Humans domesticated dogs. But cats chose to be domesticated. When people started to use agriculture for food production, they built granaries to store grain. Mice and rats moved into the granaries. There was an abundance of food for them. It was their paradise.

When cats moved into the granaries as well to hunt the mice and rats, the humans were very pleased. Some children found baby kittens and picked them up to pet them. These kittens became so used to the children that they would follow them. They became the first domesticated cats.

Unlike the dog, the cat refused to be ordered around. It was the cat who gave orders to the humans.

When our children were young in North Bay we discovered that a red tabby cat would sleep in our compost heap to keep warm. We realized that the cat was homeless and surmised that it was probably abandoned. The owners probably had to move and the cat had wandered off when they were ready to depart.

My son, Carsten, started to feed it. Each day we moved the food bowl closer and closer to our front door. Finally, we put the bowl of food inside the front door. The cat slowly and cautiously came in after it. When the door closed, the cat slam dunked the door. It hurled itself at the door over and over again. We opened the door and it ran outside.

The next morning the cat was meowing right outside the door. It seemed to say, "I thought it over. I am hungry. I am ready to come inside for food."

The cat came in to eat, and we left the door open so that he would feel comfortable. After eating, he went back outside.

The cat moved in and stayed with us. We named him Cedar because his colour and markings resembled the colour and markings of a cut cedar log. He remained somewhat aloof.

After a while, we moved to a new house and took Cedar with us. Cedar was so pleased that we took him with us that we became his people. We were now family. He would hop into bed with us and purred when Brenda would hold one of his paws.

At the new house we had a tenant living upstairs named Hans Alesi. Hans was the trainer of the Canadian women's kick boxing champion, and he held four black belts in martial arts. Hans would teach us Tai Chi in the backyard.

One day, while we were practicing Tai Chi, Hans pointed out that our cat, Cedar, was also doing Tai Chi. Cedar had a sparring partner; a chipmunk. The cat was sitting on his hind legs with his chest raised and his paws were doing the Tai Chi moves. The chipmunk was also sitting on his hind legs with his chest raised and also using his front legs for Tai Chi moves. It would also, once in a while, give a little hop.

Cedar had a sparring partner

From then on, when we were doing Tai Chi, Cedar also did Tai Chi with his friend, the chipmunk. When it became winter, Cedar caught his friend and took him inside. Then, Cedar and the chipmunk practiced Tai Chi in our basement.

One day, we found the chipmunk dead. Cedar was very sad and depressed. He looked up at me and said, "I accidentally killed my friend".

There are places where people go to watch large trained cats; lions and tigers. These trainers make friends with their big cats.

Some trainers get into the cage of a tiger and play with it. It probably started when the tiger was a cub. I have occasionally heard that a tiger had killed its trainer. That is awful. I believe

that these are accidents. I think that the tiger did not turn on its trainer. I think the trainer was accidentally killed in play just like Cedar accidentally killed his friend chipmunk.

15. BIRDS

A flock of birds in Africa

Most people like to hear birds singing. We call it singing while the birds call it talking to each other.

Bald eagle

An eagle's yell is hard to describe. Some call it a scream, which it is not. Some have described it as a screaming whistle.

Song birds live in forests and there, they can not readily see each other. Therefore, they talk out loud (yell, scream, sing, chatter). They have to be heard by their mates, chicks, and flocks.

A song thrush

The corvids (rooks, crows, ravens, magpies, jackdaws, jays, treepies, and nuthatches) are the most intelligent of birds. Their brain to body ratio is equal to that of the great apes and cetaceans (whales and dolphins). It is only a little smaller than the human brain to body size. Birds are smarter than most humans realize.

Many people put out bird feeders and some make houses for the birds to nest in. Some people form societies called 'bird watchers'. But away from human habitats, birds do not like any animal getting close to their babies. Nesting birds with young chicks have been known to attack people.

When I was a teenager on our family farm I observed a couple of barn swallows attack a big hawk driving the hawk away from their nest. The swallows were more agile and faster than the hawk. They would dive at the hawk again and again. They also landed on the back of the flying hawk and pecked away at its back. They kept this up until the hawk had been chased away.

I have also watched birds drive a cat away from their nest with young. The two birds (barn swallows) dived at the cat's head. Each time the bird either gave the cat a peck or tried to do so. The cat, unable to defend itself, walked deliberately along until it was out of the bird territory.

There have been several reports of people walking in nature when suddenly a bird swooped down and attacked them. The bird usually attacked the person's head. Many times the person attacked was confused not knowing the reason for the attack.

Scott Lenhart from the Lenape National Wildlife Refuge Complex has stated, "This is common red-winged blackbird behavior. Males are vigorously defending breeding territories and will continue to do so until all the chicks have left the nests, typically in mid-to-late July. The issue seems to be more common when jogging/walking trails border or bisect red-winged blackbird habitat."

If you do go hiking during the bird breeding season, some wildlife agencies recommend that you wear a hat.

The nest, it is a hub of communication when the chicks inhabit it. The chicks are arguing and yelling for food. If a predator comes in sight, the mother tells her kids to be very quiet.

Bird communications begin before the babies have hatched. Bird embryos chat with each other while still in the egg. After my parents bought their farm, they started their flock of chickens by buying fertilized eggs and incubating them. I would spend some time watching them every day. One day, the eggs were peeping just like young baby chicken chicks. I called my mother to hear this noise. She smiled and said, "Yes that means they will hatch in just a few days now."

A few days later, when I watched them hatch, they were peeping to each other as they were pecking their way through their shells.

Bird embryos chat with each other, using vibrations, while still inside the egg. As a result, they know when it's safe to hatch or if they should bide their time in the comfort and relative safety of their shells.

A team of biologists from Spain's University of Vigo carefully gathered sea bird eggs and organized them into test groups under incubators. They subjected one group to regular parent's predator alarm call. They placed another batch of eggs in a sound proof box.

The eggs were later returned to a common incubator. The eggs that had been exposed to the alarm calls vibrated more than the others. The vibrations were caused by the embryos wriggling nervously in their shells due to having heard the alarm calls. This caused a reaction among the eggs which had not been exposed to the alarm calls. The unborn chicks were communicating with each other. The newborns emerged in a state of caution.

Compared to a control group of eggs, they took longer to shed their shells and remained in a state of caution. They remained quieter and crouched down more often. They also showed signs of pre-induced anxiety such as higher levels of stress hormones and fewer copies of mitochondrial DNA per cell.

The unhatched birds had communicated valuable information to each other.

A crow

Crows and other corvids gather around a dead flock mate and study it. Then, they bring grass or twigs and cover it. They seem to hold a funeral service.

A cockatiel can get its owner's attention by imitating an i-phone. They are able to accurately imitate the i-phone's ring tone.

The Danish Ornithological Association has reported that in Denmark birds are singing mobile phone ring tones. At one time it was on the main Danish News channel. The main birds doing this were starlings. Thrushes were not doing it.

Musician Hollis Taylor has been studying bird songs in Australia since 2002. She started wondering whether bird songs were just messages to stake out territory, and information about food and danger. She has observed birds teaching their young how to sing. She began asking biologists whether birds sang just messages or whether they would sing just to create music. One biologist stated that as birds learn from and mimic each other, this passing of learning from one generation to the other fits the definition of culture. Being that it is culture, that makes it music.

Some birds can learn to talk like humans. In nature, parrots talk to each other.

They have a very well-developed language. The young chick is given a name at birth. The parrot is known by this name all its life.

Parrots have come to our civilization from the illegal pet trade, and they wind up in pet stores. A pet parrot just bought from the pet store will utter screams and squawks. It is really calling out the name of its mate. They mate for life and the parrot is. therefore, very upset to be missing its mate.

When the parrot learns human speech, people say, "Oh it is just parroting what it hears."

However, "Polly wants a cracker." really does mean "May I have some food please".

Ravens talk a lot better than parrots.

A Danish Raven
(As told by my mother when I was a little boy in Denmark)

There was a widower named Jensen. He found that going to work and keeping house was too much for him. So, he hired a live in house keeper. The house keeper was always complaining. Several times a day she said, "I feel so ill, Mr. Jensen."

A raven

One day, the house keeper found an injured raven. She took it in and nursed it back to health. When the raven had recovered, it flew off into the forest.

A hunter went into the forest and shot the raven. The hunter's name was also Jensen. He walked over to the raven. The raven looked up at him and said, "I feel so ill, Mr. Jensen."

The hunter picked up the raven, carried it home and nursed it back to health. When the raven had recovered it flew back to the forest. The hunter never shot another raven.

CASPER

In 1975, my brother-in-law, Willy, lived in downtown North Bay, Ontario, Canada. He found an injured raven. He decided to nurse it back to health. The raven was hopping around on his porch when the police arrived. They told him that he could not keep a raven loose. Willy put the raven in a cage. Then, two game wardens came to his house and told him that he was not allowed to keep a raven caged.

Then, Willy brought the raven to our place. We lived just outside of North Bay. At that time, my wife and I had two little girls, aged 2 and 4. The raven would hop all around in our house. He got along very well with our dog and two girls. We talked with him and he talked to us. We named him Casper. When he was well, he flew away.

The next morning, there was a tapping on our kitchen window. I went to the window and there was Casper. I opened the window. Casper said, "Good morning" and hopped into the kitchen where we fed him breakfast.

Casper said, "Good morning"

After eating breakfast he flew away.

The next morning, there was a tapping at the window. I opened the window. Casper said, "Good morning" and hopped in for breakfast. Now this happened every morning.

One day, I was working in the garden. Casper came flying and landed on my shoulder. I stopped working and walked around with Casper on my shoulder, and we had a great conversation.

Casper continued to come and sit on my shoulder every once in a while. At this time, there was an insurance agent who kept pestering us to buy insurance that we did not want. One day, the insurance agent drove into our driveway, got out of his car and started to walk towards me. Casper arrived and landed on his shoulder. The insurance agent was horrified. He was so terrified that he ran to his car and drove off. We never heard from him again.

We really enjoyed our association with this raven.

16. ARTIFICIAL COMMUNICATION

Using robots, scientists have allowed two very different species to talk to one another. The research team managed to get bees located in Austria to communicate with fish living in Switzerland.

A robot of each species was assembled. Telecommunication between the robots was used to communicate. The bee robots vibrated, changed temperature, and produced air movements. The fish robot could change its color, shape, and how it moved.

Each robot recorded the sounds made by its species and transmitted it to the other robot. Each robot then transmitted the sounds it received. They were communicating over a distance of 700 kilometers.

The two species started to change their behavior and adopted the other species characteristics. The bees became a little more restless and less likely to swarm together. The fish started to group together more than they usually would.

After 25 minutes the two groups of animals had synchronized. The fish began swimming around in their tank in a counterclockwise direction. The bees swarmed around one of their robotic terminals. Through their shared communication the two groups gradually came to a shared decision.

Francesco Mondada, a professor at BioRob, stated that the robots acted as if they were negotiators and interpreters in an international conference.

Fish and bees are not the only ones using artificial communication. The emerging field of "molecular communications" has given rise to the possibilities of monitoring diseases using a simple app.

Researchers are developing genetically engineered nanomachines that diagnose and treat disease from the inside of the body. The natural nanomachines would enter the body, non-invasively, through inhalation or swallowing and, once inside, would combat chronic illnesses such as Alzheimer's, diabetes and Crohn's disease. Commands would be sent to cells or to tiny devices operating inside the body from an operator on the outside.

The nanodevices inside the body would be connected to a kind of tattoo interface on the skin. The tattoo will gather information from inside the body and convert it into electro-magnetic waves.

Physicians could access this information via a secure network. They could assess what's happening inside the body and communicate with the nanodevices to command them to act accordingly.

A scientist in Ireland is working on manipulating DNA strands, by folding them into shapes, almost like origami, so that they can be used in their new shape to join together into the DNA of diseased cells and kill them. A gel with the nanomachines carrying the DNA is injected into the site of a tumour.

There have been relatively few biological diseases that have been undertaken using molecular communication. However, more and more work is being done every day. They are currently working on nanodevices designs that are been inserted into glioblastoma patients after their surgery in order to prevent the cancer from reoccurring. The researchers are waiting to see if it's successful.

Ultimately, researchers would like to see nanomachines work inside the body automatically. A person would simply swallow some water containing the engineered cells that had been manufactured in the lab. These cells would last a long time in the body and would give the person's body what it needs to defeat the disease.

Prof. Ian Akylidiz, from the Georgia Institute of Technology, says "I expect that automatization will be between 2025 and 2030."

"The ultimate goal is to make nanomachines operate inside the body automatically," Akylidiz says. "It would be the ultimate in personal medicine as nanomachines could be designed to suit the needs of a particular person. And, it's not far off."

17. SUMMARY

All living creatures communicate. While I was working as a biologist, other biologists sometimes talked about anthropomorphism (assigning human attributes to animals). These biologists were very much against this, and said that they hated movies which employed this motif such as "Bambi" and "Watership Down".

Biologists have been warned against having assumptions that animals share any of the mental, social, and emotional capacities of humans. However, Charles Darwin in his book, "The Expression of Emotions in Man and Animals", expressed that animals share these attributes with man. In this book, Charles Darwin stated, "Even insects play together, as has been described by that excellent observer, Huber who saw ants chasing and pretending to bite each other like so many puppies."

My study on communications in nature has shown that animals not only communicate with each other but do indeed share mental, social, and the emotional capacities that we humans possess.

Louis Leakey, the paleo anthropologist had three graduate students who studied the great apes. In the 1960s, Jane Goodall studied chimpanzees, Diane Fossey studied gorillas, and Birute Galdikas studied orangutans. These three biologists were all accused of using anthropomorphism in the results of their studies. All three became science outcasts because of their descriptions of the great apes in the field.

Their works were eventually accepted. It is now more widely accepted that empathy has an important part to play in research. De Waal has written, "to endow animals with human emotions has long been a scientific taboo. But if we do not, we risk missing something fundamental about both animals and us."

Alongside this, has come the increasing awareness of the linguistic ability of the great apes, and that they are tool makers and have culture.

The veterinarian, Bruce Folge, in his writings about cats, stated, "both humans and cats have identical neurochemicals and regions in the brain responsible for emotion. Therefore, it is not anthropomorphic to credit cats with emotions.

It has been established that animals have emotions. It is not anthropomorphic for animals to communicate their emotions. The mental, social, and emotional capacities of humans is not unique to humans. We share these things with all animals. Not only do all animals have emotions, all animals want to be loved.

REFERENCES

MNN (July 23, 2019) "Baby Birds Communicate With Each Other Before They Even Hatch"
Retreived from
https://www.mnn.com/earth-matters/animals/stories/baby-birds-communicate-eggs-hatch

Tim Richardson (May 11, 2001) "Birds Sing Mobile Phone Tunes"
Retreived from
https://www.theregister.co.uk/2001/05/11/birds_sing_mobile_phone_tunes/

Brian Koerber (December 18, 2017) "This Bird Sings The iPhone Ringtone When It Gets Upset"
Retreived from
https://mashable.com/2017/12/18/bird-cockatiel-singing-iphone-ringtone/

Hollis Taylor (December 22, 2018) "Is Birdsong Music?"
Retreived from
https://www.abc.net.au/radionational/programs/scienceshow/is-birdsong-music/10639616

Ryan F. Mandelbaum (July 22, 2019) "Gull Embryos Might Communicate With Each Other Through Their Shells"
Retreived from
https://gizmodo.com/gull-embryos-might-communicate-with-each-other-through-1836580326

Ryan F. Mandelbaum (July 17, 2019) "You Only Have Yourself To Blame If A Bird Attacks You "
Retreived from
   https://gizmodo.com/you-only-have-yourself-to-blame-if-a-bird-attacks-you-1836464595

Mark Terry (June 26, 2019) "Studying Cell Communication in Real Time Leads to Practical "Cell-Less" Therapy "
Retreived from
   https://www.biospace.com/article/observing-cells-communicate-in-real-time/

University of Groningen. "New compound allows bacterial communication to be controlled by light." ScienceDaily. ScienceDaily, 15 April 2019.
Retreived from
   https://www.sciencedaily.com/releases/2019/04/190415143925.htm

Seán Duke (June 27, 2019) "Nanomachines set out on a fantastic voyage "
Retreived from
   https://www.irishtimes.com/news/science/nanomachines-set-out-on-a-fantastic-voyage-1.3932108

Susan Brink (December 13, 2018) "A Virus can Eavesdrop On Bacterial Communication"
Retreived from
   https://www.npr.org/sections/goatsandsoda/2018/12/13/676389858/a-virus-can-eavesdrop-on-bacterial-communication

Velemir Ninkovic (July 9, 2019) "Plant-plant Communication for Sustainable Pest Management "
Retreived from
https://www.openaccessgovernment.org/sustainable-pest-management/68799/

Elizabeth Pennisi (September 13, 2018) "Plants communicate distress using their own kind of nervous system "
Retreived from
https://www.sciencemag.org/news/2018/09/plants-communicate-distress-using-their-own-kind-nervous-system

University of Würzburg (June 14, 2019) "Exciting plant vacuoles: Researchers shed new light on plant communication via electrical signals "
Retreived from
https://phys.org/news/2019-06-vacuoles-electrical.html

Andrew Masterson (March 13, 2019) "Tiny insects use a form of Snapchat"
Retreived from
https://cosmosmagazine.com/biology/tiny-insects-use-a-form-of-snapchat

Alfredo Carpineti (March 22, 2019) "Robots Allow Fish And Bees To Communicate With Each Other For The First Time"
Retreived from
https://www.iflscience.com/technology/robots-allow-fish-and-bees-to-communicate-with-each-other-for-the-first-time/

Matt Blois (January 27, 2017) "Fish communicate through their urine"
Retreived from
https://www.sciencemag.org/news/2017/01/fish-communicate-through-their-urine

Rion Nakaya (July 31, 2019) "The Wood Wide Web: How trees secretly talk to and share with each other"
Retreived from
https://thekidshouldseethis.com/post/the-wood-wide-web-how-trees-secretly-talk-to-and-share-with-each-other

Robert Mcfarlane (August 7, 2016) "The Secrets of the Wood Wide Web"
Retreived from
https://www.newyorker.com/tech/annals-of-technology/the-secrets-of-the-wood-wide-web

Joanna Klein (July 25, 2019) "Tree Stumps Are Dead, Right? This One Was Alive"
Retreived from
https://www.nytimes.com/2019/07/25/science/tree-stump-alive.html

Belden C. Lane (July 25, 2019) "Trees communicate with one another. I'm trying to listen."
Retreived from
https://www.christiancentury.org/article/first-person/trees-communicate-one-another-i-m-trying-listen

Jeffrey Lockwood (November 25, 2011) "Do Bugs Feel Pain?"
Retreived from
https://blog.oup.com/2011/11/bug-pain/

Mazza, C. A., Zavala, J., Scopel, A. L., & Ballaré, C. L. (1999). Perception of solar UVB radiation by phytophagous insects: behavioral responses and ecosystem implications. Proceedings of the National Academy of Sciences of the United States of America, 96(3), 980–985. doi:10.1073/pnas.96.3.980
Retreived from
https://www.ncbi.nlm.nih.gov/pmc/articles/PMC15336/

CARSTEN R. JORGENSEN

ABOUT THE AUTHOR

Carsten Jorgensen dedicated thirty years in studying and managing fisheries for the Ontario Ministry of Natural Resources.

Upon graduation from Queen's University in Kingston, Ontario in 1966, he accepted a biologist position on Lake Temagami with the Ontario Department of Lands and Forests.

In 1968 he also started work on Lake Nipissing. In 1970, Mr. Jorgensen was working full time as the Lake Nipissing Fisheries Assessment Unit Biologist.

In 1970 he married Brenda Black, daughter of Ontario Conservation Officer, Gordon Black.

In 1996 he retired and now enjoys spending his time playing chess, playing darts, doing Tai Chi, and writing books.

OTHER TITLES BY CARSTEN R. JORGENSEN

If you enjoyed this book by Carsten R. Jorgensen, you may also enjoy these other books that he has written:

The Saga Kings -
ISBN-13: 978-09949338-0-5

Trying To Work For The M.N.R. -
ISBN-13: 978-0-9949338-1-2

My World War Two Adventures In Denmark -
ISBN-13: 978-0-9949338-2-9

One School, Two School, Old School, New School -
ISBN-13: 978-0-9949338-3-6

Spiritual Encounters And Other Strange Stories From The Little Red School-House -
ISBN-13: 978-0-9938776-3-6

Fishes Of Lake Nipissing -
ISBN-13: 978-0-9949338-4-3

Dragons Of The World And Where They Roam -
ISBN-13: 978-0-9949338-5-0

Myths, Mythology, and Faith -
ISBN-13: 978-0-9949338-6-7

Recent Extinctions -
ISBN-13: 978-0-9949338-7-4

Or check out his author profile on Good Reads for any new and upcoming books he may be working on:

www.goodreads.com/author/show/14680643.Carsten_R_Jorgensen

www.ingramcontent.com/pod-product-compliance
Lightning Source LLC
Chambersburg PA
CBHW072210270326
41930CB00011B/2602